Tell Mommy or Daddy or Somebody

Someone Will Listen

Someone Will Help

Written by Kathy Jardine & Ashley MacCallum
Illustrated by Roberto González Lara

Copyright 2021 by Ashley MacCallum, Kathy Jardine and Kare Kids Books - All rights reserved

No part of this publication or the information in it may be quoted from or reproduced in any form by means such as printing, scanning, photocopying, or otherwise without prior written permission of the copyright holder.

Disclaimer and terms of use:
An effort has been made to ensure that the information in this book is accurate and complete, however the author and the publisher do not warrant the accuracy of the information within the book due to the rapidly changing nature of science, research, known and unknown facts, and the Internet.

The Author and the publisher do not hold any responsibility for errors, omissions, or contrary interpretation of the subject matter herein. This book is presented solely for motivational and informational purposes only.

www.karekidsbooks.ca

This book is dedicated to all the children who have found, or will find, the courage to tell Mommy or Daddy or Somebody.

When you were a baby, sometimes you cried because you were telling Mommy or Daddy or somebody that you needed something and someone listened.

They might have fed you, changed you or held you and this made you happy.

When you feel upset, sick, lonely or sad, tell Mommy or Daddy or somebody.

Someone will listen. They will do whatever they can to make you feel better.

If someone calls you names, hits you or pushes you down, tell Mommy or Daddy, your teacher or somebody right away.

Someone will help. The person who hurt you will get in trouble and they will feel bad that they did that to you and they won't hit you or call you names anymore.

If anybody ever touches you in a way that makes you feel bad, uncomfortable or upset, tell Mommy or Daddy or somebody, someone will listen. It is not your fault.

Mommy or Daddy or somebody will help to make sure that the person who made you feel bad, uncomfortable or upset won't be able to do that to you again.

Anytime somebody tells you, "This is our secret. Don't tell Mommy or Daddy or anybody," the first thing you should do is tell Mommy or Daddy or somebody.

Someone will listen, they will be glad that you told them and they will help you as needed.

Now that you have learned to always tell Mommy or Daddy or somebody, pass the message along and teach your friends to always tell Mommy or Daddy or somebody if any of these things happens to them.

Someone will listen. Someone will help.

About the Authors:
Kathy has dedicated much of her professional life helping children in need. Kathy and her daughter, Ashley, write children's books to teach valuable lessons and encourage children to be their best.
They believe that teaching children at a young age through creative means such as books is a great way to set these beautiful little people up for a life of happiness and success. Passing along messages of hope, inspiration and encouragement is what keeps these creative Authors passionate about what they do.

Kare Kids Books

Karekidsbooks@gmail.com

Illustrations and book formatting by Roberto González
rogolart.com | roberto@rogolart.com

www.ingramcontent.com/pod-product-compliance
Lightning Source LLC
Chambersburg PA
CBHW081423080526
44589CB00016B/2654